Daily Language Review

WEEK 1 — Monday

Correct these sentences.

1. duz his cuzin lives in unother sity

   _____

2. After james and tim cleened the garage grandma gave them five dollars

   _____

Singular or plural?

3. cattle _____

Circle the word in each row that is spelled correctly.

4. oxigun   oxegun   oxygen
5. umpare   umpire   umpyre

Daily Language Review

WEEK 1 — Tuesday

Write an antonym for each word.

1. demolish _____
2. imaginary _____

Correct these sentences.

3. the Childrens valubles were storeed in the teachers closit

   _____

4. that Hot Rod is the noisier vehicul on my Block

   _____

Declarative, interrogative, imperative, or exclamatory?

5. Who's your favorite music artist? _____

Daily Language Review

WEEK 1 Wednesday

Correct these sentences.

1. wernt their no milk in the refrijerator

   _____

2. there going to come to sea me at 7 pm

   _____

Choose the best word to complete this analogy.

3. heavy : light :: near : _____

   close   far   next door   traveled

Where would the following probably take place?

4. The boy watched from the terminal as the commuter plane landed on the runway.

   _____

Write the root or base word.

5. illogical _____

Daily Language Review

WEEK 1 Thursday

Write the correct abbreviation.

1. Avenue _____

2. pound _____

What print reference source would you use to find the meaning of *thesaurus*?

3. _____

Correct these sentences.

4. lets play a game of Soccor to day

   _____

5. antonio was to big for his bike sew he sold it at red barn flee market

   _____

Daily Language Review

Friday

Use the comparative or the superlative form of the word in parentheses to complete each sentence.

1. (tall) Suzi was the _____ player on the basketball team.

2. (heavy) Mark is _____ than Steve.

3. (hard) This is the _____ homework I've had all year.

4. (busy) Every Saturday morning, the mall is the _____ place in town.

5. (long) Most snakes are _____ than worms.

Daily Language Review

My Progress

How many did you get correct each day? Color the squares.

	Monday	Tuesday	Wednesday	Thursday	Friday
5					
4					
3					
2					
1					

Daily Language Review

WEEK 2 — Monday

Correct these sentences.

1. my Dad gave the prezint two pete and I
_____

2. it werent no serprize I new he wood do it
_____

Use context clues to determine the meaning of the bolded word.

3. The timeline gave the events in **chronological** order.
_____

Fact or opinion?

4. Over 75 percent of the students had a library card. _____

5. Every student should read one book each month. _____

Daily Language Review

WEEK 2 — Tuesday

Write a synonym for *succeeded*.

1. _____

Circle the word that comes first in alphabetical order.

2. fiber   feverish   festive   fervor   fertilize

Correct these sentences.

3. aprul is my faverutest month of the year
_____

4. we mayd the last paiment on hour new computor
_____

Write the pronoun that would replace the underlined nouns.

5. <u>Bernie</u> and <u>Ben</u> went orienteering with the Scouts. _____

Daily Language Review

WEEK 2 — Wednesday

Correct these sentences.

1. the work men layed a straite track for the frayt train

   _____

2. maggie claymd she wuz to busy to dew her home work

   _____

Name this part of a friendly letter.

3. Your pen pal, _____

Simile or metaphor?

4. The butterfly was as graceful as a ballerina. _____

Circle the adverb in this sentence.

5. Touch the new puppy gently so you don't injure it.

Daily Language Review

WEEK 2 — Thursday

Circle the word that comes last in alphabetical order.

1. shale   shaft   shady   shallot   shaky

How many syllables does this word have?

2. relationship _____

Correct these sentences.

3. mrs peters asked mr beckman will the concert start at 700 or 730

   _____

4. the workmen has come to fix the oven in sammys kitchin

   _____

Complete the word to make the /l/ sound.

5. sever _____

Daily Language Review

WEEK 2 Friday

Add a suffix to each of these words to answer the clue.

1. One who studies plants and animals   biolog _____

2. Not taking care as you work   care _____

3. One who does not tell the truth   li _____

4. In an unusual manner   strange _____

5. Being filled with a feeling of joy   joy _____

Daily Language Review

WEEK 2 My Progress

How many did you get correct each day? Color the squares.

	Monday	Tuesday	Wednesday	Thursday	Friday
5					
4					
3					
2					
1					

Daily Language Review

WEEK 3 Monday

Correct these sentences.

1. we had a flat tire amos wuz sun burned and we got losted

2. chris thought I hope thay will chose me for there teem

Circle the correct abbreviation for *Doctor*.

3. Doc   Dr   Dr.   none of these

Write the correct salutation for a business letter to the doctor, Ben Corliss.

4. _____

Write the meaning of this idiom.

5. Winning the race was quite a feather in my cap.

Daily Language Review

WEEK 3 Tuesday

Synonyms or antonyms?

1. arrival, departure _____

2. abandon, discontinue _____

Correct these sentences.

3. look out below he called that rock is falling

4. mother and her polish friend mrs. slovik went to a chinese resterant

Circle the word that does not belong in this group.

5. granite   quartz   feldspar   gasoline   amber

Daily Language Review

WEEK 3 Wednesday

Correct these sentences.

1. my friend mr. murphy visited churchs in canada china and japan

   _____

2. there mom ask them to go to blacks market for her

   _____

Circle the cause and underline the effect.

3. The campers had to be rescued after they wandered off the trail and became lost.

Singular or plural?

4. phenomena _____

Write the past tense of the verb *teach*.

5. _____

Daily Language Review

WEEK 3 Thursday

Write the contraction that is made from these two words.

1. will not _____

What print reference source would you use to find several synonyms for *walked*?

2. _____

Correct these sentences.

3. why due I have to due my home work now asked tori

   _____

4. its best to get you're work done before you watch tv said mom

   _____

Rewrite this word, adding a prefix.

5. appoint _____

Daily Language Review

WEEK 3 Friday

Read the following paragraph and decide if the underlined parts have a capitalization error, a punctuation error, a spelling error, or no error.

Ancient Egypt a rich and prosperous nation depended on farming. The crops growen by farmers
 　　　　　　　　1　　　　　　　　　　　　　　　　　　　　　　　　　　　　2

living in the nile valley fed and clothed Egypt's people. Farmers raised cattle geese oxen and
　　　　　3　　　　　　　　　　　　　　　　　　　　　　　　　　　　　4

pigs. They planted wheat, flax, and a variety of fruits and vegetables.
　　　　　　　　　　　　　　　　5

1. _____
2. _____
3. _____
4. _____
5. _____

Daily Language Review

WEEK 3 My Progress

How many did you get correct each day? Color the squares.

	Monday	Tuesday	Wednesday	Thursday	Friday
5					
4					
3					
2					
1					

Daily Language Review

WEEK 4 — Monday

Correct these sentences.

1. on april 2 grandma avery will celebrate her hundred birthday
   _____

2. i studied an interesting artical kayaking in alaska in world magazine
   _____

Write the past tense of the verb *grow*.

3. _____

Write a fact about *Canada*.

4. _____

Circle the antonym for *pursue*.

5. chase   continue   abandon   study

WEEK 4 — Tuesday

Choose the best word to complete this sentence.

1. She _____ have any coins in her pocket.
   don't   doesn't   never   always

Correct these sentences.

2. the old tyred dog wantz to lay down by the warm fire
   _____

3. are we suppose to read the plains or the desert in are books
   _____

Write the two words that make up this contraction.

4. you'd _____   _____

Use this homophone pair in one sentence: *forth, fourth*.

5. _____

Daily Language Review

WEEK 4 — Wednesday

Correct these sentences.

1. the scaryest story in *horrifying tales* was sounds by t s jones

2. the farmer let 'em ride him horse

Circle the adjectives in this sentence.

3. The graceful antelope leaped quickly over the rough, rocky roadbed and disappeared into the thick bushes beyond.

Write two words that rhyme with *thrown*.

4. _____   _____

Circle the word that is spelled correctly.

5. receive   receve   recieve   receeve

Daily Language Review

WEEK 4 — Thursday

Circle the word that comes first in alphabetical order.

1. myth   mystery   myself   mysterious

Where is someone who is saying the following?

2. "Due to unexpected turbulence, the captain has turned on the Fasten Seatbelt sign."

Correct these sentences.

3. dad sets in a chair to read him newspaper

4. is miss browns english class gonna resight robert frosts poem

Which part of speech is underlined: noun, verb, adjective, or adverb?

5. Lay the new clothes <u>neatly</u> on the bed before you go outside. _____

Daily Language Review

WEEK 4 — Friday

Combine the following sentences to make one sentence.

1. The dog chased the cat. The cat ran up the tree.

2. Seline needed to buy a new dress. Seline was performing in a concert.

3. Tom and Seth hit home runs. The team won the championship game.

4. Would you like some lemonade to drink? Would you like some cookies to eat?

5. I am very hungry. I think I could eat a horse.

Daily Language Review

WEEK 4 — My Progress

How many did you get correct each day? Color the squares.

	Monday	Tuesday	Wednesday	Thursday	Friday
5					
4					
3					
2					
1					

Daily Language Review

WEEK 5 — Monday

Correct these sentences.

1. "carl will you help me do home work afterschool"
   _____

2. "no not today because I'm going somewhere with my mom"
   _____

Rewrite this phrase, using a possessive noun.

3. the video game belonging to Scott _____

Choose the best word to complete this sentence.

4. _____ going to meet us in the lobby after the movie.
   Their   There   They's   They're

What is the meaning of this figure of speech?

5. When I asked her for a loan, she said, "Go fly a kite."
   _____

Daily Language Review

WEEK 5 — Tuesday

Circle the correct way to divide this word into syllables.

1. rep re sen ta tive   re pre sent a tive   rep re sent a tive

Does the underlined adverb tell how, when, where, or to what extent?

2. A cheetah runs the most <u>quickly</u> of all cats. _____

Correct these sentences.

3. why duznt he ever due his home work
   _____

4. it don't look like any thing ive seen before said dr thomas
   _____

Circle the cause and underline the effects.

5. The lava oozed down the sides of the volcano, and black smoke smothered the sunlight after the eruption.

Daily Language Review

WEEK 5 — Wednesday

Correct these sentences.

1. after im done skateing ill go to the liburary four a hour

2. did you get a letter from youre pen pal

Which part of speech is underlined: noun, verb, adjective, or adverb?

3. The <u>flickering</u> candles stood at attention in the frosting drifts. _____

Synonyms or antonyms?

4. reluctant, eager _____

Circle the correct abbreviation for *Michigan*.

5. MIC   MI   MN   MH

WEEK 5 — Thursday

Write the past and future tenses of the verb *drip*.

1. Past: _____   Future: _____

Rewrite this phrase, using a possessive noun.

2. the tusks and ears of the elephant _____

Correct these sentences.

3. we stoped to use the bathroom stretch and eat diner

4. two boys bikes was left in the senter of fivth street on friday aprl 1

Declarative, interrogative, imperative, or exclamatory?

5. I went to the soccer game with Leon last Saturday. _____

Daily Language Review

WEEK 5 — Friday

Circle the best word to complete each analogy.

1. *Cub* is to *lion* as *foal* is to _____.
       colt   dog   zebra   monkey

2. *Hat* is to *head* as *lid* is to _____.
       jar   cover   hair   beret

3. *Picture* is to *frame* as *cream* is to _____.
       butter   cup   pitcher   whipped

4. *Dog* is to *leash* as *balloon* is to _____.
       cloud   branch   helium   string

5. *Tennis* is to *racket* as *volleyball* is to _____.
       net   hand   basket   court

Daily Language Review

WEEK 5 — My Progress

How many did you get correct each day? Color the squares.

	Monday	Tuesday	Wednesday	Thursday	Friday
5					
4					
3					
2					
1					

Daily Language Review

WEEK 6 Monday

Correct these sentences.

1. mrs lee have traveled to europ asia and south america

_____

2. i cant weight to travel by myself

_____

Use context clues to determine the meaning of the bolded word.

3. Climbing to the rock ledge will test his skills and his **mettle**.

_____

Write two synonyms for *mistaken*.

4. _____   _____

Fiction or nonfiction?

5. Unopened flower buds of the clove tree are used to dull the pain of a toothache, freshen breath, and flavor ham. _____

WEEK 6 Tuesday

Does the underlined adjective tell which one, what kind, or how many?

1. Carlos exclaimed, "Look at that <u>huge</u> pumpkin!" _____

Circle the predicate in this sentence.

2. The whiskers on my kitten twitch when I rub its back.

Correct these sentences.

3. derek sad he was two busy too make his bed

_____

4. bob lee and al went to the steinhart aquarium to see the shark

_____

Circle the word that is not spelled correctly.

5. inconsiderate   uncomfortable   prejudice   preveiw

Daily Language Review

WEEK 6 Wednesday

Correct these sentences.

1. every saterday myh brother watches *iron chef*

   _____

2. last sumer my friend tara moved to taos new mexico

   _____

Choose the best word to complete this analogy.

3. seldom : many :: often : _____

   lots   more   few   several

Synonyms, antonyms, or homophones?

4. quick, speedy _____

5. week, weak _____

WEEK 6 Thursday

Write the contraction that is made from these two words.

1. we are _____

Rewrite this word, adding a prefix.

2. test _____

Correct these sentences.

3. if we work hard replied judy well earn a good grade

   _____

4. michael ask how soon will brakefast be ready

   _____

Past, present, or future?

5. occupied _____

Daily Language Review

WEEK 6 Friday

Circle the correct word to complete each sentence.

1. How _____ did you do on the test?   good   well
2. _____ puppies are growing bigger every day.   Are   Our
3. _____ that woman standing by the car?   Who's   Whose
4. Do you know _____ jacket that is?   who's   whose
5. When _____ the book reports due?   are   our

Daily Language Review

WEEK 6 My Progress

How many did you get correct each day? Color the squares.

	Monday	Tuesday	Wednesday	Thursday	Friday
5					
4					
3					
2					
1					

Daily Language Review

WEEK 7 Monday

Correct these sentences.

1. that john elway football belongs to my brother and I
   _____

2. michael and me ran in the big brothers marathon
   _____

Use these three homophones in one sentence: *there, their, they're.*

3. _____
   _____

Circle the preposition in this sentence.

4. A young boy is hurrying along the crowded sidewalk.

Write a word that would belong in this group.

5. speak   utter   verbalize   inform   _____

Daily Language Review

WEEK 7 Tuesday

Write an antonym for this word.

1. ancient _____

Circle the word that is not spelled correctly.

2. wrestle   whistel   knapsack   scratch

Correct these sentences.

3. every one were invited to there party
   _____

4. several butterflys and eagels flew over head
   _____

Does this word have a suffix or a prefix?

5. impolite _____

Daily Language Review

WEEK 7 — Wednesday

Correct these sentences.

1. them womens lunchs all cost the same amoount

   _____

2. jim likes apple cherry and peach pie but I only like cake

   _____

Write the root or base word.

3. prehistoric _____

Simile or metaphor?

4. When the principal walked by, Sam sat as still as a statue. _____

Is *after* used as a preposition or an adverb in this sentence?

5. After the farmer harvested the corn, he sold it as ensilage. _____

WEEK 7 — Thursday

Write the number of syllables in each word.

1. inconvenient _____

2. inconsiderate _____

Correct these sentences.

3. mi sister teared off the books cover

   _____

4. park city hired a couch for the boys sports teams

   _____

Write the pronoun that would replace the underlined words.

5. The soldiers and their prisoners marched in single file. _____

Daily Language Review

WEEK 7 Friday

Match the words with the correct definitions.

1. intersection   a. the rate at which something happens

2. vertical   b. a mathematical statement

3. equation   c. straight up and down

4. currency   d. a place where one thing crosses another

5. frequency   e. the money used in a country

Daily Language Review

WEEK 7 My Progress

How many did you get correct each day? Color the squares.

	Monday	Tuesday	Wednesday	Thursday	Friday
5					
4					
3					
2					
1					

Daily Language Review

WEEK 8 — Monday

Correct these sentences.

1. please tell me the answer to the riddel begged jose
   _____

2. will you help them guys paint there fence
   _____

Is the comma used correctly? Circle *yes* or *no*.

3. August 31, 2009   Yes   No

4. Salina Kansas, 76532   Yes   No

Which part of speech is underlined: noun, verb, adjective, or adverb?

5. We offer the largest <u>selection</u> of cool beverages, tasty meals, and luscious desserts in town.
   _____

WEEK 8 — Tuesday

Choose the best word to complete this analogy.

1. leaf : spinach :: root : _____
   flower   carrot   tomato   lettuce

Correct these sentences.

2. jeff sits his glasses on the tabel
   _____

3. I need to right a thank you note for the gift my aunt sent me
   _____

Use the context clues to determine the meaning of the bolded word.

4. The party next door was a big **distraction** as I tried to concentrate on my homework.
   _____

Fact or opinion?

5. It is important to protect forests and wildlife at any cost. _____

Daily Language Review

WEEK 8 — Wednesday

Correct these sentences.

1. we read articles form newsweek time and cricket
   _____

2. while she pourd tea the girl spilt it on he mothers desk
   _____

Circle the word that comes first in alphabetical order.

3. feminine   fellowship   femoral   feline

Circle the word that is spelled correctly.

4. neithur   worrys   gratious   siege

Circle the adjectives in this sentence.

5. The fierce winds surged across the carefully planted wheat fields.

Daily Language Review

WEEK 8 — Thursday

Name this part of a friendly letter.

1. Your friend, _____

What do the words in this group have in common?

2. biology   chemistry   anatomy   nuclear physics
   _____

Correct these sentences.

3. whil I weighted for the griddel to git hot I drawded a desighn
   _____

4. the sky opened up and rein slamed to the grownd
   _____

Write the contraction that is made from these two words.

5. must not _____

Daily Language Review

WEEK 8 Friday

Read the following paragraph and decide if the underlined parts have a capitalization error, a punctuation error, a spelling error, or no error.

<u>The kendo competition</u> was about to begin <u>at the Obon Festival.</u> In traditional dress, the
    1   2

competitors moved like <u>frajle dancers</u> around the ring. <u>Briefly lunging toward</u> each other and
                        3   4

then stepping back the competitors performed. <u>Watch the graceful warriors fencing.</u>
                                                             5

1. _____
2. _____
3. _____
4. _____
5. _____

Daily Language Review

WEEK 8 My Progress

How many did you get correct each day? Color the squares.

	Monday	Tuesday	Wednesday	Thursday	Friday
5					
4					
3					
2					
1					

Daily Language Review

WEEK 9 Monday

Correct these sentences.

1. whose that there boy over their

    _____

2. after the hen lies her eggs she sets on them

    _____

Write a word that would belong in this group.

3. lakes   rivers   oceans   ponds   _____

What is personified in the following sentence?

4. The books on my shelf whispered secrets as I tried to go to sleep.

    _____

Circle the word that is not spelled correctly.

5. orchestra   ordinery   dictionary   stare

Daily Language Review

WEEK 9 Tuesday

Rewrite this sentence, adding at least one adjective.

1. The puppy wagged its tail.

    _____

What is the correct way to divide these words into syllables?

2. obstinate _____

3. occupant _____

Correct these sentences.

4. me and pete got a new dog at adams pet shop

    _____

5. tim's shews are two big sew he will by a knew pare at ace shoestore

    _____

Daily Language Review

WEEK 9 — Wednesday

Correct these sentences.

1. the new deskes in the class room belong to ana todd and kate

_____

2. uncle fred bot us pizza at freddies

_____

Is the bolded word a subject pronoun or an object pronoun?

3. The teacher trusted **him** to take attendance. _____

Choose the best word to complete this analogy.

4. *Predator* is to *prey* as *owl* is to _____.
    fly   mouse   hawk   talons

Combine these two ideas into a single sentence.

5. Susan got out of bed. She looked out her window to check the weather.

_____

_____

WEEK 9 — Thursday

Circle the correct abbreviation for *Road*.

1. R.   Rd.   RD.   Rd

Rewrite each word, using the suffix *-ing*.

2. receive _____ worry _____ plan _____

Correct these sentences.

3. constantly tom worrys about his end of the year projeckt

_____

4. the thersty boy drank the dr pepper in one swallough

_____

Synonyms or antonyms?

5. irregular, rough _____

Daily Language Review

Friday

Read the paragraph. Underline the topic sentence and write the main idea. Then list three supporting details under the main idea.

Some seeds move on the wind. They have winglike parts to catch the wind. Other seeds have hooks or stickers. They catch in the fur of animals and are carried to new places. Some seeds float on water to new places. People move seeds, too. They plant them in their yards and gardens. Seeds travel in many different ways.

Main Idea: _____

_____

Details: 1. _____

2. _____

3. _____

Daily Language Review

My Progress

How many did you get correct each day? Color the squares.

	Monday	Tuesday	Wednesday	Thursday	Friday
5					
4					
3					
2					
1					

Daily Language Review

WEEK 10 Monday

Correct these sentences.

1. native americans beleived that spirits protected them

2. there was hundreds of tribes in america when christopher columbus landed

Fact or fantasy?

3. People and animals can sink in quicksand. _____

Choose the best word to complete each sentence.

4. The trumpet's range is _____ than the baritone's.
   higher   highest   high   none of these

5. The tuba's range is _____ of all.
   lower   lowest   low   none of these

WEEK 10 Tuesday

Write an opinion about *pollution*.

1. _____

If the guide words on a dictionary page are *penicillin* and *pepper*, which word would not be on the page?

2. peninsula   peony   penniless   peppermint   people

Correct these sentences.

3. i have the adresses of frends living in other countrys

4. mrs moores busnesses is taking pitchers of familee groups

Use this homophone pair in one sentence: *for, four*.

5. _____

Daily Language Review

WEEK 10 Wednesday

Correct these sentences.

1. the climit along the equator is diffrent from the climit in alaska

2. his vehicul had a puntured tire and sew he waited by the syde of the rode

Write the present tense of the verb *caught*.

3. _____

Declarative, interrogative, imperative, or exclamatory?

4. Watch out for the hole in the deck. _____

Underline the subject in this sentence.

5. How many purchases were made on Sunday?

Daily Language Review

WEEK 10 Thursday

Circle the word that comes last in alphabetical order.

1. shudder   shuffle   shut   shutdown   shuttle

Write the plural of each noun.

2. fox _____   wolf _____

Correct these sentences.

3. mr tuttle asked did you studee four you're math test

4. I spended a day at the libary writing my essae for english

Write the complete predicate of this sentence.

5. Our friendship has lasted a long time, despite our differences.

Daily Language Review
Week 10 — Friday

What do the underlined phrases mean?

1. Mrs. Peters said that the new easel would <u>fill the bill</u>.

2. My grandpa is nearly ninety, but he's <u>fit as a fiddle</u>.

3. The custodian said that she'd <u>get to the bottom</u> of the graffiti on the wall.

4. Lance has <u>his finger in every pie</u>.

5. Your dad will never double your allowance. <u>Get real!</u>

Daily Language Review
Week 10 — My Progress

How many did you get correct each day? Color the squares.

	Monday	Tuesday	Wednesday	Thursday	Friday
5					
4					
3					
2					
1					

Daily Language Review

Monday

Correct these sentences.

1. the words impolight and inkonsiderate are close in meaning

    _____

2. dr landrys motto is always bee prepeared

    _____

Rewrite this word, using a suffix.

3. strange _____

Simile or metaphor?

4. Her hair was as shiny as a blackbird's wing. _____

Write a word that would belong in this group.

5. calm   soothe   still   allay   _____

Daily Language Review

Tuesday

Circle the words in each row that rhyme.

1. cruel   school   tell   cool   rule   role
2. chute   newt   shut   route   suit   stool

Correct these sentences.

3. "well dew you think you can help me on saterday"

    _____

4. "i can help you monday jay if thats not to layt"

    _____

Write a sentence about *wheels* that contains an example of alliteration.

5. _____

Daily Language Review

WEEK 11 Wednesday

Correct these sentences.

1. all the ice in the lemonaide begun to disapear
   _____

2. the jelly in slim's sandwitch driped out onto hiz shirt
   _____

Circle the words that have four syllables.

3. representative   technology   currency   substituted

Circle the cause and underline the effect.

4. The ticket line was so long that we missed the first part of the movie.

Write a common noun for each proper noun.

5. Mr. Beckman _____   Arlington, Virginia _____

Daily Language Review

WEEK 11 Thursday

Write the comparative and superlative adjectives for *heavy*.

1. Comparative: _____   Superlative: _____

Synonyms, antonyms, or homophones?

2. substitute, switch _____

Correct these sentences.

3. we catch that there bus at the corner of elm street and first avenue
   _____

4. traveler airlines allows you to take one suit case and a carry on bag
   _____

Choose the best word to complete this sentence.

5. The _____ of his aftershave lingered in the room.
   cent   scent   sent

32

Daily Language Review

WEEK 11 — Friday

Write each of these suffixes next to its meaning below.

    ly   less   ar   ful   ment   or

1. full of _____

2. the condition of _____

3. without _____

4. in what manner _____

5. one who _____

Daily Language Review

WEEK 11 — My Progress

How many did you get correct each day? Color the squares.

	Monday	Tuesday	Wednesday	Thursday	Friday
5					
4					
3					
2					
1					

Daily Language Review

WEEK 12 Monday

Correct these sentences.

1. the paddel boats moved along the missouri river

2. land ahoy the first mate shouted

Use the context clues to determine the meaning of the bolded word.

3. Although he'd never signed an agreement, his **tacit** understanding of the law was clear.

Circle the word that is spelled correctly.

4. amphibean   enviroment   performance   temperature   campain

Circle the adjectives in this sentence.

5. The heavily armored crocodile slid slowly from the mossy banks into the dark depths.

WEEK 12 Tuesday

What part of speech is underlined?

1. Can an amphibian live <u>in an environment</u> where the temperature is very low?

Correct these sentences.

2. we wont have an asignment untill wedsday september 3

3. they're were three peaces of pizza on the plait kelly took the larger one

Circle the prepositions in this sentence.

4. I went to the soccer game with my friend Leon.

Write a synonym for this word.

5. stalk _____

Daily Language Review

WEEK 12 — Wednesday

Correct these sentences.

1. six geeses was searching for sum delishush worms to eat

2. last year we spended our vacashion at uncle jims farm

Choose the best words to complete this analogy.

3. jack : flat tire :: hammer : _____
   dull pencil   broken window   deflated ball   loose board

Choose the best word to complete this sentence.

4. _____ your closest living relative?
   Whose   Who's   Who

Circle the adverb in this sentence.

5. Several flew overhead.

WEEK 12 — Thursday

Fact or opinion?

1. Water expands when it is frozen. _____

Are the underlined words a common noun or a proper noun?

2. The students swarmed across the playground and splashed into the <u>community pool</u>.

Correct these sentences.

3. The hail stones pounded the roofs during the storem

4. dr rivers standed besighed his pateinces bed and said say ahhhh

Write an antonym for *rude*.

5. _____

Daily Language Review

WEEK 12 Friday

**Read the words in each line and mark *sentence* or *not a sentence*.
In each line, circle the subject and underline the predicate.**

1. Climbed the mountain and camped   ○ sentence   ○ not a sentence

2. The machine responded to his command   ○ sentence   ○ not a sentence

3. Always in motion and chattering too, the young toddler   ○ sentence   ○ not a sentence

4. Tom, Franco, Seline, and Julie played   ○ sentence   ○ not a sentence

5. He lurched and stumbled against the table   ○ sentence   ○ not a sentence

---

Daily Language Review

WEEK 12 My Progress

How many did you get correct each day? Color the squares.

	Monday	Tuesday	Wednesday	Thursday	Friday
5					
4					
3					
2					
1					

Daily Language Review

Week 13 — Monday

Correct these sentences.

1. werent their no cookies left

   _____

2. hello out there terrys voice was muffled by his mask

   _____

Circle the preposition in this sentence.

3. Two delivery trucks pulled into the parking lot.

Choose the best word to complete this sentence.

4. Do you know the recipe very _____?
   easy   good   well   none of these

Divide this word into syllables.

5. standardize _____

Daily Language Review

Week 13 — Tuesday

Choose the best word to complete this analogy.

1. *Shallow* is to *deep* as *imaginary* is to _____.
   make-believe   fiction   authentic   hard-headed

Are the underlined words the subject or the predicate?

2. The outcome of the game depends on us. _____

Correct these sentences.

3. why cant he never git here on thyme

   _____

4. the singers will end the show with there version of its a small worlde

   _____

Fact or opinion?

5. Honey is a nutritious natural food. _____

Daily Language Review

WEEK 13 — Wednesday

Correct these sentences.

1. the sioux lived on the great plains and trackt bufalo

_____

2. woodland tribes like the onondaga maid they're homes of wood

_____

Complete this analogy.

3. *cm* is to *centimeter* as *yd* is to _____.

Circle the word that is not spelled correctly.

4. distruction   division   infection   attention   description

Write a pronoun that would replace the underlined noun.

5. The <u>custodians</u> worked hard to get ready for the open house. _____

Daily Language Review

WEEK 13 — Thursday

Write the contraction that is made from these two words.

1. they are _____

What print reference source would you use to find out about the world's largest volcanoes?

2. _____

Correct these sentences.

3. whos going to kollect the six oclock male when its delivred

_____

4. ive know idea what your talking about

_____

Write a synonym for *cruel*.

5. _____

Daily Language Review

WEEK 13 Friday

Read the following paragraph and decide if the underlined parts have a capitalization error, a punctuation error, a spelling error, or no error.

The first olympic games were held in Olympus Greece, in 776 B.C. Todays Olympic
       1   2   3

competitions include many different sports. Approximatly 10,500 athletes participated in the
                                                                               4

2008 Summer Games in Beijing.
              5

1. _____
2. _____
3. _____
4. _____
5. _____

Daily Language Review

WEEK 13 My Progress

How many did you get correct each day? Color the squares.

	Monday	Tuesday	Wednesday	Thursday	Friday
5					
4					
3					
2					
1					

Daily Language Review

WEEK 14 Monday

Correct these sentences.

1. my most faverit candys are miad out of swiss chocalate

2. borises baby sister torn the libray book pages

Write the base or root word.

3. condensation _____

What is the meaning of this figure of speech?

4. That game is for the birds. I wish we could get a new one.

Write the complete subject of this sentence.

5. The stunt diver used an oxygen tank until he reached the surface.

Daily Language Review

WEEK 14 Tuesday

Write the plural form of this noun.

1. radius _____

Choose the best words to complete this sentence.

2. When I go to _____ aquarium, I always take _____ guidebook to help me identify the fish.
                a an   a an

Correct these sentences.

3. the dogs owners writed a pome about they're pet

4. can you play quiet untill the meeting is adjurned

Write the comparative and superlative adjectives for *handsome*.

5. Comparative: _____ Superlative: _____

Daily Language Review

WEEK 14 Wednesday

Correct these sentences.

1. h w longfellow wrote listen my children and you shall here of the mid-night ride of paul revere

2. the wether caster toled the temperture explaned the fog and gave a forecaste

Use context clues to determine the meaning of the bolded words.

3. The volunteers were always willing to **step into the breach** and offer assistance to the tornado victims.

Write the past tense of these verbs.

4. bind _____

5. weep _____

Daily Language Review

WEEK 14 Thursday

Is the bolded letter a subject pronoun or an object pronoun?

1. The teacher and **I** presented the awards at the assembly. _____

What part of speech is underlined in this sentence?

2. Green grasshoppers <u>gracefully</u> glide in gravity-defying leaps. _____

Correct these sentences.

3. I will lie the photograf on that table in plane view

4. flowers of every color bloomd in professer shaws garden

What is the meaning of this figure of speech?

5. I'll tell you where Mom keeps the cookies, but you've got to <u>keep it under your hat</u>.

Daily Language Review

WEEK 14 Friday

Combine the sentences to make one sentence.

1. The football team ran onto the field. They carried their helmets in their hands.

2. Pam found a book for her report. She used the library browser on the computer. Pam checked out the book.

3. Tom fell off the bike. He learned that racing bikes can be dangerous.

4. Ahmad is our new student body president. He got the most votes in the election.

5. Ashley lives next door to me. She feeds my puppies when I'm gone.

Daily Language Review

WEEK 14 My Progress

How many did you get correct each day? Color the squares.

	Monday	Tuesday	Wednesday	Thursday	Friday
5					
4					
3					
2					
1					

Daily Language Review

Week 15 Monday

Correct these sentences.

1. due you think mr long will except my report if its hand written
   _____

2. my grandad believes you shuld always carry a hankercheif
   _____

Circle the preposition in this sentence.

3. Students use spoken and written language for many different purposes.

Simile or metaphor?

4. I wandered across the meadow, a lonely cloud in a clear blue sky. _____

Circle the words that are not spelled correctly.

5. several   numerel   vowal   hundred   toward

Daily Language Review

Week 15 Tuesday

Choose the best word to complete this analogy.

1. down : pillow :: beans : _____
   beanstalk   beanie   bed   beanbag

Circle the correct abbreviation for *Boulevard*.

2. Bvd.   blvd   Blvd.   bd

Correct these sentences.

3. if I was a docter I wood help people stay well
   _____

4. county hospital is located on the corner of king way and state street
   _____

Past, present, or future?

5. wander _____

Daily Language Review

WEEK 15 Wednesday Name:

Correct these sentences.

1. my brothers bestest riddle is what kind of house ways the least

2. the anser is a lite house

What do the words in this group have in common?

3. rectangle   trapezoid   square   triangle   parallelogram

If the guide words on a dictionary page are *hungry* and *hyacinth*, which words would not be on the page?

4. hurl   hydrangea   hustle   hunger   hutch

Does the underlined adverb tell how, when, where, or to what extent?

5. Tommy quickly ran <u>behind</u> the house. _____

Daily Language Review

WEEK 15 Thursday

Does this word have a prefix or a suffix?

1. misunderstand _____

Write the singular form of this noun.

2. halves _____

Correct these sentences.

3. mrs turlock says that I must learn how to use parenthesis

4. I cant imagin a more ridiculus idea

Synonyms or antonyms?

5. free, restricted _____

44

Daily Language Review

WEEK 15 Friday

Identify the subject and verb or verbs in each sentence.

1. She crept past the baby's crib.

    Subject: _____   Verb(s): _____

2. She loved to walk in the rain.

    Subject: _____   Verb(s): _____

3. Toby gave his mother the report.

    Subject: _____   Verb(s): _____

4. Tomorrow I'd like to leave early.

    Subject: _____   Verb(s): _____

5. The three girls smiled and clapped their hands.

    Subject: _____   Verb(s): _____

Daily Language Review

WEEK 15 My Progress

How many did you get correct each day? Color the squares.

	Monday	Tuesday	Wednesday	Thursday	Friday
5					
4					
3					
2					
1					

Daily Language Review
WEEK 16 — Monday

Correct these sentences.

1. scott make your arms slice into the water shouted couch storm

2. he reminded him keep your kick going strong out of you're turns

Circle the cause and underline the effect.

3. I didn't understand the questions on the test because I missed the previous class.

Add the correct punctuation to this business greeting.

4. To Whom It May Concern

Use this homophone pair in one sentence: *billed, build*.

5. _____

Daily Language Review
WEEK 16 — Tuesday

If the guide words on a dictionary page are *feedback* and *fencing*, which words would be on the page?

1. feel   feeble   felon   fence   fender

Correct these sentences.

2. I all ready finishd doing the dishus mom sighed

3. please she said put your dirtee plait on the drain bored before you leaf

Write the root or base word.

4. effective _____

Write the plural form of this noun.

5. sandbox _____

Daily Language Review
WEEK 16 — Wednesday

Correct these sentences.

1. the waitriss said to day we have strawberrys raspberrys and blackberrys

   _____

2. wood you like some whipt cream with you're berrys she asked

   _____

Declarative, interrogative, imperative, or exclamatory?

3. Look out below! _____

Is the bolded word a subject pronoun or an object pronoun?

4. Hot or cold, **they** tasted great! _____

Circle the words that have three syllables.

5. entrance   entertain   envision   enviable   envelope

Daily Language Review
WEEK 16 — Thursday

What print reference source would you use to find the boundary between Egypt and Israel?

1. _____

Real or make-believe?

2. The cheetahs ran free in the Kenyan game park while tourists watched from their jeeps.

   _____

Correct these sentences.

3. the baby looked like shes going to ball

   _____

4. the baby sitter ask do you have any ideas about what we shud do

   _____

What part of speech is underlined?

5. The cheering crowd <u>roared</u> as the ball cleared the fence. _____

Daily Language Review

WEEK 16 Friday

Write the verb forms for each verb.

	Present	Past	Past Participle (used with *has*, *had*, or *have*)
1.	am	_____	_____
2.	come	_____	_____
3.	do	_____	_____
4.	eat	_____	_____
5.	see	_____	_____

Daily Language Review

WEEK 16 My Progress

How many did you get correct each day? Color the squares.

	Monday	Tuesday	Wednesday	Thursday	Friday
5					
4					
3					
2					
1					

Daily Language Review

WEEK 17 Monday

Correct these sentences.

1. at midnight wee heared jims frends searching for snacs in the cuboard

2. how meny cartens comed in the maail shipmant this after noon

Are the underlined words part of the subject or part of the predicate?

3. Lay the baby in her crib <u>so she can take a nap.</u> _____

Add punctuation to this address.

4. 5430 Broad Ave #310

   Oakland CA 94618

Write an opinion about *endangered species*.

5. _____

Daily Language Review

WEEK 17 Tuesday

Write the two words that make up this contraction.

1. there've _____ _____

Synonyms or antonyms?

2. surpass, exceed _____

Correct these sentences.

3. who's dog are them over their

4. I wish I cud stay at home too meat you but I have two go

Underline the prepositional phrase in this sentence.

5. Carla's friend Margo came for a long visit.

Daily Language Review

WEEK 17 — Wednesday

Correct these sentences.

1. nurse nancy gived her a cleen bandadge four her kne
   _____

2. it may not seem write but its all ways been the rule
   _____

Complete this analogy.

3. *Minute* is to *clock* as *ounce* is to _____.

Choose the best word to complete this sentence.

4. Yesterday he _____ his hat on the peg by the door.
   hang   hanged   hung   will hang   has hung

Use this homophone pair in one sentence: *wood, would*.

5. _____

WEEK 17 — Thursday

Circle the word that is not spelled correctly.

1. multiply   currency   vertical   manufacture   atmophere

Proper noun or common noun?

2. the priest _____

3. Father McGovern _____

Correct these sentences.

4. i cant weight to try the snacks nicole made cake sara made candy and bob made pie
   _____

5. farmer ted dug a whole in hiz garten for a compost pit
   _____

Daily Language Review

WEEK 17 Friday

Write the plural of each noun. Then write how you made the word plural.

1. president _____

2. bench _____

3. variety _____

4. journey _____

5. life _____

Daily Language Review

WEEK 17 My Progress

How many did you get correct each day? Color the squares.

	Monday	Tuesday	Wednesday	Thursday	Friday
5					
4					
3					
2					
1					

Daily Language Review
Week 18 Monday

Correct these sentences.

1. sasha whispered to her self where did john hid moms ring

2. i read to chapters of *tom sawyer* every knight before I go two bed

Use context clues to determine the meaning of the bolded word.

3. My older sister is always running into things because she is **oblivious** to her surroundings.

Choose from these words to complete the sentence: *ware, wear, where.*

4. _____ can Teresa find a costume to _____ to the party?

If the guide words on a dictionary page are *ringing* and *ripple*, which word would be on the page?

5. ringed   rind   rinsing   rise   riptide

Daily Language Review
Week 18 Tuesday

Write the correct contraction for *of the clock*.

1. _____

Use this homophone pair in one sentence: *attendance, attendants.*

2. _____

Correct these sentences.

3. the dishs on the shelfs fell during the earth quake

4. the mountian in the paynting is mtt hood said the museum giude

Identify this part of a business letter.

5. The Western Stage
   165 Homestead Street
   Tyler, Texas 03673 _____

Daily Language Review
Week 18 — Wednesday

Correct these sentences.

1. mrs springs drys flowcres for bouguets

   _____

2. the park acrosst the street from mi house is called central park

   _____

Is the bolded word a subject pronoun or an object pronoun?

3. Did you see **her** wave her hand? _____

Fact or opinion?

4. Mayan architects were some of the world's best builders. _____

Do the underlined adjectives tell which one, what kind, or how many?

5. <u>Lacy</u> curtains were draped across the <u>clear</u> glass of the windows.

   _____

Daily Language Review
Week 18 — Thursday

Is the underlined word a common noun or a proper noun?

1. The <u>captain</u> readied the plane for takeoff. _____

Declarative, interrogative, imperative, or exclamatory?

2. Before a big test, is it more important to sleep or study? _____

Correct these sentences.

3. aunt jo had to fly to denver on her weigh to st louis

   _____

4. put extra rightin paper scissor pencils and glue in the tub

   _____

Synonyms, antonyms, or homophones?

5. affirm, deny _____

Daily Language Review

WEEK 18 Friday

Read the following paragraph and decide if the underlined parts have a capitalization error, a punctuation error, a spelling error, or no error.

The spoted salamander remains almost unchanged from the first salamander that walked on The
    1   2   3
Earth about 330 Million years ago. It lives in caves, under rocks, and logs, and moves only
               4   5
during the blackest hours of the night.

1. _____
2. _____
3. _____
4. _____
5. _____

Daily Language Review

WEEK 18 My Progress

How many did you get correct each day? Color the squares.

	Monday	Tuesday	Wednesday	Thursday	Friday
5					
4					
3					
2					
1					

Daily Language Review

WEEK 19 — Monday

Correct these sentences.

1. noone in the familee had ever bin to hawaii

2. how meny boxs of cookys did you sell the troop leader ask

Does the underlined adverb tell how, when, where, or to what extent?

3. The man danced <u>gracefully</u> across the floor. _____

Choose the best word to complete this sentence.

4. The hen named Peanut laid _____ eggs last month than the one named Annie.
    few   less   fewer   lesser

Circle the correct way to divide this word into syllables.

5. lia bil i ty   li abil i ty   li a bil i ty   li a bil it y

---

WEEK 19 — Tuesday

Choose the best word to complete this analogy.

1. *Opaque* is to *transparent* as *turmoil* is to _____.
    peaceful   turbulent   stormy   clear

Circle the word that does not belong in this group.

2. oak   maple   pine   geranium   elm

Correct these sentences.

3. to me new years day means grandmas chili and a family feast

4. the principle said make sure your children has a quite time for home work

Declarative, interrogative, imperative, or exclamatory?

5. The shark in the aquarium's tank is well-fed. _____

Daily Language Review
WEEK 19 — Wednesday

Correct these sentences.

1. the cup shood be levil when you pore the punch warned mom
   _____

2. i cant beleive i won the jack pot carlos screamed
   _____

Write the past tense of the verb *fight*.

3. _____

Singular possessive or plural possessive?

4. the centipede's feet   _____

5. the boys' team   _____

Daily Language Review
WEEK 19 — Thursday

Circle the word that is spelled correctly.

1. tomorow   terible   remember   comeing   hospitel

Write three words with the prefix *mid-*.

2. _____   _____   _____

Correct these sentences.

3. scott came home at 8 30 after the boy scout meeting
   _____

4. his friends ask mrs morrow to come to his recitle
   _____

Where would the following probably take place?

5. "Would you like to send the package priority? Do the contents need to be insured?"
   _____

Daily Language Review

WEEK 19 Friday

Combine the sentences to make one sentence.

1. My friends like to go to the gym and work out. I like to go to the gym and work out. We like to go three times a week.

2. Mr. Sutter is my coach. He believes that practice is the key to winning.

3. This morning, the bushes wore new coats of white. There was a snowstorm last night.

4. I called my grandma on the phone. When she first began talking, she sounded weak and shaky. By the time we hung up, her voice was full of life.

5. Mowing the lawn is a big job. Besides cutting the grass, you have to service the mower. Then you have to edge the sidewalk.

Daily Language Review

WEEK 19 My Progress

How many did you get correct each day? Color the squares.

	Monday	Tuesday	Wednesday	Thursday	Friday
5					
4					
3					
2					
1					

Daily Language Review

Week 20 — Monday

Circle the word in which the apostrophe is not used correctly.

1. we'll   mightn't   she'll   has'nt   those'll

Correct these sentences.

2. on friday my frends and I will go two central zoo sad sue

3. "peter wood you rather sea the tigger the lion or the chimp"

What function do the underlined words in this sentence have?

4. The Mayans may <u>have transported</u> stones over long distances when they built their temples.

Write the plural form of this noun.

5. tomato _____

Week 20 — Tuesday

Simile or metaphor?

1. The baby's hair was corn silk against her soft pink face. _____

Circle the word that is not spelled correctly.

2. guessed   enough   supposed   poison   insted

Correct these sentences.

3. there weding cayk was sew tall it almost reached the sealing

4. the brides vale borrowed from her aunt lookt like a shiney cloud

Use context clues to determine the meaning of the bolded word.

5. Everyone brought something to eat, so we had a **bountiful** amount of food for the potluck.

Daily Language Review

WEEK 20 Wednesday

Correct these sentences.

1. in my room ive displayt mi collecktion of caps from evry baseball team

2. its fun to wear one and amagine your self at bat facing randy johnson

What print reference source would you use to find the street address of your local pizza parlor?

3. _____

What does the abbreviation *misc.* stand for?

4. _____

Circle the cause and underline the effect.

5. When Thutmose II died, his son was too young to assume the responsibilities of a pharaoh, so his wife Hatshepsut became pharaoh instead.

Daily Language Review

WEEK 20 Thursday

Circle the word that comes last in alphabetical order.

1. disprove   dissatisfy   dissolute   dissent   dissection

Write a homophone for the word *piece*.

2. _____

Correct these sentences.

3. my uncle one the distinguished flying cross for his bravry

4. were all very prowd of hiz specil distincshun

Circle the words that are adverbs.

5. pretty   there   swam   softly   until

59

Daily Language Review

WEEK 20 Friday

What do the underlined phrases mean?

1. Thomas <u>lost his temper</u> for no reason.

   _____

2. I <u>got cold feet</u> when it came time to <u>take the stage</u>.

   _____

3. I can't go to the game today, but <u>I'll take a rain check</u>.

   _____

4. Sadi bought the used computer game <u>for a song</u>.

   _____

5. She was <u>skating on thin ice</u> when she stepped over the guardrail to take a photograph.

   _____

Daily Language Review

WEEK 20 My Progress

How many did you get correct each day? Color the squares.

	Monday	Tuesday	Wednesday	Thursday	Friday
5					
4					
3					
2					
1					

Daily Language Review

WEEK 21 — Monday

Correct these sentences.

1. can you come over to watch *jeopardy* asked jamal
   _____

2. my mom is out of town so ill ask grandpa travis answered
   _____

Circle the cause and underline the effect.

3. Archaeologists believe that around 1400 B.C., some great disaster struck the palace at Knossos; they found smoke stains on the walls, as well as scattered vessels.

Circle the best word to complete this sentence.

4. Steven has _____ three inches in the last six months.
         groan   grown

Circle the antonyms in this sentence.

5. If you do a thorough job of research, you will find that writing a conclusion is much easier than if you do an incomplete job and don't understand your subject.

Daily Language Review

WEEK 21 — Tuesday

Name: _____

Choose the best word to complete this sentence.

1. It's my job to make sure that the floor has been _____.
      sweeped   sweped   swept   swepted

Circle the words that have the same sound as /ow/ in *now*.

2. couch   allow   throw   house   trout   bough

Correct these sentences.

3. teresa will pick-up the papers sweep and dust
   _____

4. what dew you want too be responsibul four ask mrs timms
   _____

Fact or fantasy?

5. When the water evaporated, it became invisible vapor. _____

Daily Language Review
WEEK 21 — Wednesday

Correct these sentences.

1. them players choosed mr rupp as the best basket ball couch
   _____

2. hav you every heared the beatles song yellow submarine
   _____

What is the present tense of the verb *spoke*?

3. _____

If the guide words on a dictionary page are *stringent* and *structure*, which words would not be on the page?

4. string   stripe   strong   stroke   struggle   strident

Choose the best word to complete this analogy.

5. *Fish* are to *creel* as *strawberries* are to _____.
   shortcake   pudding   basket   field

Daily Language Review
WEEK 21 — Thursday

Name: _____

What is the object of this sentence?

1. Grandma bought Whitney a puzzle with over 1,000 pieces. _____

Where is someone who sees the following?

2. The captains meet at midfield for the coin toss before the kickoff.
   _____

Correct these sentences.

3. sydney asked will we sea sharks at ocean world
   _____

4. after school I saw peter who asked can you stop buy my house
   _____

Write the root or base word.

5. contradiction _____

Daily Language Review

Week 21 — Friday

Choose the best word to complete each sentence.

1. He _____ seen walking by the pond yesterday.
   is   been   was

2. When _____ you think you will finish the book report?
   does   do   don't

3. Bill, please give this cup of tea to _____.
   him   them   he

4. How many _____ were exhibited at the fair?
   sheep   sheeps   sheep's   sheepes

5. _____ going to the ballgame?
   Whose   Who's   Who   Whom

Week 21 — My Progress

How many did you get correct each day? Color the squares.

	Monday	Tuesday	Wednesday	Thursday	Friday
5					
4					
3					
2					
1					

Daily Language Review

WEEK 22 Monday

Correct these sentences.

1. josh tori and maddie went to disney world

2. thay road space mountain rock 'n' roller coaster and test track

Use context clues to determine the meaning of the bolded word.

3. Jeremy took some time to **contemplate** the question before he answered it.

Circle the words that are spelled correctly.

4. manufacture   volenteer   charecteristic   civilization   infectted

Is the underlined word singular possessive or plural possessive?

5. The <u>women's</u> room is down the hall. _____

WEEK 22 Tuesday

Circle the adjectives in this sentence.

1. Mouth-watering aromas seeped from Mother's oven and made my hungry stomach rumble.

Circle the word that comes last in alphabetical order.

2. guava   guest   guardsman   guise   guile

Correct these sentences.

3. if you join the book club you will recieve a prescription to *highlights*

4. perks supreme is the only koffee that my mother like

Underline the prepositional phrases in this sentence.

5. After the service, all of his relatives went to the restaurant.

Daily Language Review

WEEK 22 Wednesday

Correct these sentences.

1. if we go to study hall now dave boasted well be finished first

   _____

2. huck finn is a ficshunel charactr created by mark twain

   _____

Write the correct abbreviation for *September*.

3. _____

Rewrite this word, adding a suffix.

4. state _____

What is the subject of this sentence?

5. Will you be able to get your homework done on time? _____

WEEK 22 Thursday

Write synonyms and antonyms for these words.

1. accurate   Synonym: _____   Antonym: _____

2. glamorous   Synonym: _____   Antonym: _____

Correct these sentences.

3. meekers student council voted to visit hospitals on thanksgiving

   _____

4. the teachers will go two ralphs to by the food

   _____

Divide this word into syllables.

5. mosquito _____

Daily Language Review

WEEK 22 Friday

Label the subject and verb or verbs in each sentence.

1. Ted's puppy wagged its tail and barked.

    Subject: _____ Verb(s): _____

2. Slippery Rock is the name of a town.

    Subject: _____ Verb(s): _____

3. The squirrel gathered nuts and stored them in its cheeks.

    Subject: _____ Verb(s): _____

4. How did you do on the test?

    Subject: _____ Verb(s): _____

5. Summer vacation is almost here.

    Subject: _____ Verb(s): _____

Daily Language Review

WEEK 22 My Progress

How many did you get correct each day? Color the squares.

	Monday	Tuesday	Wednesday	Thursday	Friday
5					
4					
3					
2					
1					

Daily Language Review

WEEK 23 Monday

Correct these sentences.

1. keli and glen want two go horse back riding on friday at 3 o clock

   _____

2. the smith twins sara and emily where matching outfites

   _____

Write a word that belongs in this group.

3. bang, crash, ping, splash, splat, _____

Past, present, or future?

4. When will you go to camp? _____

Name this part of a business letter.

5. I'm writing to inform you that you've been awarded the contract. _____

WEEK 23 Tuesday

Choose the best word to complete this sentence.

1. Fred is so tired, he needs to _____ down before the game.
       lay   laid   lie   lying

If the guide words on a dictionary page are *claim* and *classical*, which words would be on the page?

2. clatter   classroom   clasp   clarinet   clack   clam

Correct these sentences.

3. when im tried of writeing i stand up and breath deeply

   _____

4. often what i think i key board is not whats on the page

   _____

Synonyms or antonyms?

5. endure, persist _____

Daily Language Review

WEEK 23 Wednesday

Correct these sentences.

1. when i asked who is it i heard a voice replie its only me
   _____

2. humpty dumpty posed a impossible challenge for the kings mens
   _____

Write a fact about *homework*.

3. _____

Circle the two pairs of synonyms in this sentence.

4. I hope to locate the original deed or to at least discover the first owner's name.

Does the underlined adverb phrase tell how, when, where, or to what extent?

5. The jukebox played the song <u>over and over.</u> _____

Daily Language Review

WEEK 23 Thursday

Write the possessive noun.

1. the three dogs of Arturo _____

Use context clues to determine the meaning of the bolded word.

2. Although we can live a long time without food, water is **indispensable**.
   _____

Correct these sentences.

3. its all most lunch time shouted simon
   _____

4. hurry lets go to carpenter beach four a piknic
   _____

Does the underlined adjective tell which ones, what kind, or how many?

5. <u>Those</u> wiggly worms felt funny in my hand. _____

WEEK 23 Friday — Daily Language Review

Read the following paragraph and decide if the underlined parts have a capitalization error, a punctuation error, a spelling error, or no error.

<u>Have you ever wondered</u> where ice cream <u>came from.</u> On one of his trips to the Far East,
    1   2

Marco Polo <u>returned to italy</u> with a recipe for a <u>frozen milk desert.</u> Italy is credited with
              3   4

<u>popularising ice cream.</u>
         5

1. _____
2. _____
3. _____
4. _____
5. _____

WEEK 23 My Progress — Daily Language Review

How many did you get correct each day? Color the squares.

	Monday	Tuesday	Wednesday	Thursday	Friday
5					
4					
3					
2					
1					

Daily Language Review

WEEK 24 Monday

Correct these sentences.

1. of all the stars in the sky the sun is the closer to earth

2. its a bawl of burning gas's thats about fiv billion years old

Does the underlined adverb tell how, when, where, or to what extent?

3. Tori liked to twist her hair and pin it <u>up</u> in a knot. _____

Simile or metaphor?

4. Mrs. Perch's hair was a nest for the perky red bow. _____

Is the underlined word singular or plural?

5. Which <u>fish</u> in the aquarium swims the fastest? _____

Daily Language Review

WEEK 24 Tuesday

Is the bolded word a subject pronoun or an object pronoun?

1. We wanted to thank **them** for all of their help. _____

Correct these sentences.

2. do you think that some day sum one will travel all the weigh to mars

3. sid nose that the letter was supposd to arived on june 10 by 10 a m

What is the meaning of this figure of speech?

4. Nancy always <u>has her nose in a book.</u> _____

Circle the subject of this sentence.

5. Covered with suds and dripping with water, the toddler dashed from the bathtub to the bedroom.

70

Daily Language Review

WEEK 24 Wednesday

Correct these sentences.

1. youd beter clean up that mess quick

   _____

2. boris and jean packt the picters for the air express truck

   _____

Choose the best word to complete this sentence.

3. Scott had _____ many dirty dishes in his room.

   two   to   too   tow

Write *sentence* or *not a sentence* on the line.

4. Always busy working in the kitchen, the cooks _____

5. The computer responded to his command _____

Daily Language Review

WEEK 24 Thursday

Circle the contraction that is spelled correctly.

1. we'll   there'ell   they'are   that'ill   ther'ed

Which part of speech is underlined: noun, verb, adjective, or adverb?

2. The runner sprinted down the track <u>effortlessly</u>. _____

Correct these sentences.

3. in his poem primer lesson carl sandburg wrote look out how you use proud words

   _____

4. isnt it all most time for the asembly

   _____

Synonyms or antonyms?

5. tumult, pandemonium _____

Daily Language Review

WEEK 24 Friday

Combine the sentences to make one sentence.

1. Marilyn bought some sandals. She tried on hiking boots, walking shoes, and ballet slippers.

2. We drove to the camping store to buy a tent cover. When we got there, the store was closed.

3. The road was covered with black ice. The car turned the corner. The car slid off the road.

4. Jo went to visit her sister. Jo's sister lives in St. Louis. Jo only has one sister.

5. I found a carton of eggs in the refrigerator. It had only one egg in it. I couldn't make cookies.

Daily Language Review

WEEK 24 My Progress

How many did you get correct each day? Color the squares.

	Monday	Tuesday	Wednesday	Thursday	Friday
5					
4					
3					
2					
1					

Daily Language Review

WEEK 25 Monday

Correct these sentences.

1. these here sentenses our begining to all look a like

   _____

2. honey is a treet four bares sayed the zoo keaper

   _____

Write the possessive noun.

3. the books of the teachers _____

Use this homophone pair in one sentence: *plain, plane.*

4. _____

Fact or opinion?

5. A brainstorm is a good idea. _____

Daily Language Review

WEEK 25 Tuesday

Write the comparative and superlative forms of *quiet.*

1. Comparative: _____ Superlative: _____

Underline the nouns in this sentence.

2. The kindergartners buzzed around the soccer ball like bees around a hive.

Correct these sentences.

3. i use post it notes to lable the paiges that kneed korrections

   _____

4. after ten laps around the track his chest heaves as he breaths

   _____

Circle the correct way to divide this word into syllables.

5. en ve lop e   en vel ope   en ve lope   env el ope

Daily Language Review

WEEK 25 — Wednesday

Correct these sentences.

1. my gardner suggests i planted tulips lilacs and a rose
   _____

2. hav you had two hav you're teeth pulled buy a dentist
   _____

Choose the best word to complete this analogy.

3. *Seldom* is to *often* as *many* is to _____.
   lots   more   few   several

Suffix or prefix?

4. envious _____

5. entrust _____

Daily Language Review

WEEK 25 — Thursday   Name:

Circle the cause and underline the effect.

1. To avoid the extreme daytime heat, we drove across the desert at night.

What print reference source would you use to find a synonym for *length*?

2. _____

Correct these sentences.

3. i bought kiwi from mexico and pinapple from hawaii
   _____

4. can you git some peeches for me ask frank
   _____

Choose the correct date to complete this sentence.

5. Mrs. Ford was born on _____ at Weld County General Hospital.
   March 13 1982   March 13, 1982   March 13, 1982,

Daily Language Review

WEEK 25 Friday

Write what the underlined phrases mean.

1. Let's get down to brass tacks. How much do you want for your bike?

   _____

2. My mom gets a kick out of shopping.

   _____

3. I don't believe the salesman. He's full of hot air.

   _____

4. On the soccer field, I feel like a fish out of water.

   _____

5. His idea to start school fifteen minutes earlier every day went over like a lead balloon.

   _____

Daily Language Review

WEEK 25 My Progress

How many did you get correct each day? Color the squares.

	Monday	Tuesday	Wednesday	Thursday	Friday
5					
4					
3					
2					
1					

Daily Language Review

WEEK 26 Monday

Correct these sentences.

1. ray will pick up his new pick up at truck city tomorow
   _____

2. during the last rain storm my roof sprung a leak
   _____

Use the context clues to determine the meaning of the bolded word.

3. Kali's **charisma** made her a popular choice for class president.
   _____

Identify this part of a friendly letter.

4. Dear Aunt Betty, _____

Underline the prepositional phrase in this sentence.

5. My baby sister sits in her highchair, giggles, and throws her food overboard.

WEEK 26 Tuesday

Circle the correct abbreviation for *quart*.

1. qrt.   q.   qt.   QT

Write a proper noun for each common noun.

2. city _____

3. business _____

Correct these sentences.

4. the scott boys bike club meets on wedesday after skhool
   _____

5. wood you like to come to the next meating as my gest
   _____

Daily Language Review

WEEK 26 — Wednesday

Correct these sentences.

1. when beavers built dams everie member of an beaver family helps

    _____

2. mother father and three or for younger beavers work togather

    _____

Write the comparative and superlative adjectives of *easy*.

3. Comparative: _____   Superlative: _____

Choose the best word to complete this analogy.

4. password : computer network :: key : _____

   house   lock   ring   mouse

Write the complete subject of this sentence.

5. The transparent plastic crate held all of her photos and letters.

    _____

Daily Language Review

WEEK 26 — Thursday

Write the pronouns that would replace the underlined nouns.

<u>Megan and Chelsea</u> played on the <u>trampoline</u>.
     1   2

1. _____

2. _____

Correct these sentences.

3. they're many diffrent kinds of letus lik romaine and bibb

    _____

4. chef dennis uses for lettuce's in his famose harvest salad

    _____

Circle the cause and underline the effect.

5. Don watched a DVD on my dad's computer, so when Dad turned it on, the battery was low.

Daily Language Review

WEEK 26 Friday

Circle the best word to complete each sentence.

1. Tommy looked all over for the keys he _____.
                                              lose   losed   lost

2. Samantha _____ all the Girl Scouts her new badge.
                show   shown   showed

3. Did you know _____ both from Nebraska?
                    their   they're   there

4. Why did you _____ those cookies so close to suppertime?
                    eat   ate   eaten

5. The choir had _____ the school song at the assembly.
                    sang   singed   sung

Daily Language Review

WEEK 26 My Progress

How many did you get correct each day? Color the squares.

	Monday	Tuesday	Wednesday	Thursday	Friday
5					
4					
3					
2					
1					

Daily Language Review

WEEK 27 Monday

Correct these sentences.

1. i named my pet george because i got him at georges pet store

2. when i pet georges i says youre my bestest frend

Is the bolded word a subject pronoun or an object pronoun?

3. Will **you** dance with Mary at the recital? _____

4. Can you eat **it** and play at the same time? _____

What do these words have in common?

5. knit   crochet   cross-stitch   needlepoint

Daily Language Review

WEEK 27 Tuesday

What part of speech is underlined in these sentences?

1. The narrow road <u>twisted</u> between the tall, snowy mountains.

2. <u>Twenty-five</u> team members competed in the tournament.

Correct these sentences.

3. the navajo people are famos for there beutiful rugs

4. historyical thay livd on the southwestern planes

Synonyms, antonyms, or homophones?

5. moan, mown _____

Daily Language Review
Week 27 — Wednesday

Correct these sentences.

1. Pete finded his faverit dvd transformers under hiz bed

2. dr morgan xrayed annies teeth and said no cavitys

Rewrite the word *graph*, adding a prefix.

3. _____

Where would the following probably take place?

4. "Don't forget to write your name on your test. Show all your work."

Circle the two words that need to be switched in order to make the list in correct alphabetical order.

5. stoke   stole   stomach   stoop   stone

Daily Language Review
Week 27 — Thursday

Circle the word that is a plural noun.

1. people   dog's   dress   goes

Correct these sentences.

2. the trafik wasn't bad this mourning maybe its a holiday

3. frank complained my hands are chap becuz of the cold wet whether

Write the past and future tenses of the verb *forbid*.

4. Past: _____   Future: _____

Circle the complete subject of this sentence.

5. The enormous elephants, two fierce tigers, a gawky llama, and Bobo the trained bear shared the train car with the Flying Delaneys—all twelve of them!

Daily Language Review
Week 27 Friday

Complete each sentence, using the appropriate homophones.

(hole, whole)
1. Philip spent the _____ morning mending a _____ in his sock.

(right, write)
2. Be sure that you _____ the _____ answer for each question.

(principal, principle)
3. I set up a meeting with the _____ because I believed that the basic _____ behind the code had been violated.

(raise, raze, rays)
4. Through the bright _____ of first morning, the soldier began to _____ the new flag. At the same time, the bulldozers began to _____ the old building.

(stationery, stationary)
5. With plumed pen and embossed _____, the scribe assumed her _____ position for the diorama.

Daily Language Review
Week 27 My Progress

How many did you get correct each day? Color the squares.

	Monday	Tuesday	Wednesday	Thursday	Friday
5					
4					
3					
2					
1					

Daily Language Review

WEEK 28 Monday

Correct these sentences.

1. heather weaved a small blanket for the babies bed

2. drew knew the write anser befor the teecher had ask the queston

Use the context clues to determine the meaning of the bolded word.

3. I was **enthralled** by the book and read nonstop for hours.

Write the root or base word.

4. reconstruction _____

5. imported _____

Daily Language Review

WEEK 28 Tuesday

Circle the correct way to divide this word into syllables.

1. lum in ous   lu min ous   lu mi nous   lum i nous

Correct these sentences.

2. the ladie wavved her hand at her reltor and said we want that house

3. the house was desihnd by a famus archtekt named frank lloyd wright

Are the underlined words the subject or the predicate?

4. When evening came, the bubbling brook's babble seemed to increase in volume.

The word *reflection* has _____.

5. a prefix   a suffix   both a prefix and a suffix   neither a prefix nor a suffix

Daily Language Review

WEEK 28 — Wednesday

Correct these sentences.

1. mr gerk announcd if i don't have coffey my day is off too a bad start

   _____

2. here sir said hillary i think i can help as she heald out a steeming mug

   _____

Fact or opinion?

3. All students need foreign language training. _____

Correct the spelling of the words that are not spelled correctly.

4. athletes   chocolotes   rhythems   purchases

   _____

Circle the words that are adverbs.

5. suddenly   regrettably   hustle   soon   significant

WEEK 28 — Thursday

Does the underlined adjective tell which one, what kind, or how many?

1. Summer days are barefoot walks in cool grass. _____

2. Those mosquitoes love summer days, too. _____

Correct these sentences.

3. run six laps before comeing too class coach okeefe said

   _____

4. thirdy two differnt speeshes of birds live near lake oswego

   _____

Simile or metaphor?

5. Rain is a magic elixir that changes brown landscape to green. _____

Daily Language Review

WEEK 28 Friday

Read the following paragraph and decide if the underlined parts have a capitalization error, a punctuation error, a spelling error, or no error.

Tomas huddled <u>like a scarred animal</u> in the brush. He had come to <u>this region to give a lecture</u>
                      1   2

about using plants from the <u>amazon rainforest</u> for medical research, but now he was stranded
                                3

on <u>a deserted unpaved</u> road <u>somewhere near the equator.</u>
     4   5

1. _____
2. _____
3. _____
4. _____
5. _____

Daily Language Review

WEEK 28 My Progress

How many did you get correct each day? Color the squares.

	Monday	Tuesday	Wednesday	Thursday	Friday
5					
4					
3					
2					
1					

Daily Language Review

WEEK 29 Monday

Correct these sentences.

1. molly and max his two terriers make life exciting at joshs house

   _____

2. we read the declartion of independance in hour class

   _____

Write the comparative and superlative forms of *bad*.

3. Comparative: _____   Superlative: _____

Is it a sentence? Circle *yes* or *no*.

4. Ted at the wheel, the blue van piled with gifts for all the cousins   yes   no
5. Come here   yes   no

WEEK 29 Tuesday

Circle the cause and underline the effect.

1. Forest Service officials are combing the area for Japanese Beetle larvae. Last week, the larvae were found in a backyard garden. They are considered a danger to area vineyards.

Correct these sentences.

2. stuart little is a carring new comer to the little family

   _____

3. nashvil tennessee is the capitol of that state

   _____

Write the appropriate word in each sentence: *leased, least*.

4. He _____ the garage for the upcoming year.

5. Having a roof over his head was the _____ of his worries.

Daily Language Review
WEEK 29 Wednesday

Correct these sentences.

1. a trip to the museum of natrual history is a treet exclaimed sara

2. tomorow is my favorit song from annie

What is this part of a business letter called?

3. Sincerely,

   Tom Adams, Secretary _____

Underline the prepositional phrases in this sentence.

4. In this helter-skelter world, I need to find a place of my own quickly.

Complete this analogy.

5. foundation : cement :: skeleton : _____

Daily Language Review
WEEK 29 Thursday

Circle the correct abbreviation for *District of Columbia*.

1. Dist. of Co.   D of C   D.C.   DC

Declarative, interrogative, imperative, or exclamatory?

2. Give Sam a hand for his effort. _____

Correct these sentences.

3. imagin a arbor with roses cascading frum it's branchs

4. my garden is lik a vegetbul stand with dayly prodeuce spechuls

Circle the correct way to divide this word into syllables.

5. hea vi er   heav i er   heav ier   hea vie r

Daily Language Review

Week 29 Friday

Label the subject and verb in each sentence.

1. Pat and Mike went fishing.

    Subject: _____   Verb: _____

2. Mike brought the fishing poles.

    Subject: _____   Verb: _____

3. Pat caught the first fish.

    Subject: _____   Verb: _____

4. The fish was too small to keep.

    Subject: _____   Verb: _____

5. He threw the tiny fish back into the water.

    Subject: _____   Verb: _____

Daily Language Review

Week 29 My Progress

How many did you get correct each day? Color the squares.

	Monday	Tuesday	Wednesday	Thursday	Friday
5					
4					
3					
2					
1					

Daily Language Review

WEEK 30 Monday

Correct these sentences.

1. jose finded a wallet with recepts from a account at world bank
   _____

2. when he returnned the wallet to securitie he recieved a reward of 50 dollars
   _____

Use the context clues to determine the meaning of the bolded word.

3. The escaping robber was **encumbered** by the heavy sack of loot.
   _____

Past, present, or future?

4. Patricia can't wait for her birthday party. _____

5. Walking in the forest provided a respite in Bob's day. _____

WEEK 30 Tuesday

Fact or opinion?

1. My piano teacher can play ragtime melodies with flair. _____

Write an antonym for the word *optimistic*.

2. _____

Correct these sentences.

3. dr lee is a pediatrician who is like a grandfather to his patience
   _____

4. why didnt julie take drivers education this summer
   _____

Use this homophone pair in one sentence: *scent, sent*.

5. _____

Daily Language Review

Week 30 — Wednesday

Correct these sentences.

1. mr smith the art teacher lended me the book about picasso

2. peter and me want to try to pant a murel in picassos style

Is the underlined word a noun, verb, adjective, or adverb?

3. A threatening cloud <u>hung</u> high in the sky as we anticipated rain. _____

Circle the word that is spelled correctly.

4. weapen   secend   hospitel   happen

Does the underlined adjective tell which one, what kind, or how many?

5. <u>Shimmering</u> stars shine softly in the summer sky. _____

Week 30 — Thursday

Past, present, or future?

1. The farmer is having a sale of his farm equipment in the fall. _____

2. Colby flew to Amsterdam for Petrov's graduation. _____

Correct these sentences.

3. noises especially loud ones are frightening at night explained fred

4. my kitten ollie naps wakes up and stretches and than sleeps sum more

Write the comparative and superlative adjectives of *funny*.

5. Comparative: _____   Superlative: _____

Daily Language Review

WEEK 30 Friday

Write the letter of the meaning for each underlined word or words.

1. The police officer may <u>cite</u> you for speeding. _____

2. It was a magnificent <u>sight</u>! _____

3. Our school is to be the <u>site</u> of the filming. _____

4. The <u>sight</u> on the telescope helps the astronomer. _____

5. The boy <u>set his sights</u> on winning the trophy. _____

a. to strive for
b. a device looked through to help aim
c. summon to court
d. display
e. location

Daily Language Review

WEEK 30 My Progress

How many did you get correct each day? Color the squares.

	Monday	Tuesday	Wednesday	Thursday	Friday
5					
4					
3					
2					
1					

Daily Language Review

WEEK 31 Monday

Correct these sentences.

1. the pioneer society is a group of descendints of familys that home steaded in the west

   _____

2. my grate grandmothers parents were part of that originel settlment

   _____

Write synonyms for these words.

3. retrieve _____

4. secluded _____

Does the underlined adverb tell when, how much, or where?

5. The doctor showed patience as the traffic crawled <u>forward.</u>

   _____

Daily Language Review

WEEK 31 Tuesday

What is the meaning of this figure of speech?

1. I've got a big test tomorrow. I'd better <u>hit the books.</u>

   _____

Correct these sentences.

2. how many of there are us

   _____

3. sal and ron and me went out to hour new club house

   _____

What do these words have in common?

4. spaghetti   linguine   manicotti   ziti

   _____

5. diapers   stroller   bottles   bib

   _____

Daily Language Review

Week 31 Wednesday

Correct these sentences.

1. my little couzen always says give me 5

2. the phone rung jest as mom was leafing the house

Circle the cause and underline the effect.

3. I missed my connection in Denver due to a late takeoff in Los Angeles.

Write an opinion about *violence*.

4. _____

Circle the word that is not spelled correctly.

5. authoritative   fragmentary   presentible   fractional   prejudice

---

Daily Language Review

Week 31 Thursday

What type of job is described here?

1. He carefully checked the network organization and then installed the new hub.

Use context clues to determine the meaning of the bolded word.

2. Sugar is an **essential** ingredient in making sugar cookies.

Correct these sentences.

3. i just finished reding a book entitled through my eyes by ruby bridges

4. it descrbed her experience as the only black student in her school

Underline the complete predicate of this sentence.

5. After the false start, the swimmer dove into the water and swam to victory.

Daily Language Review

Week 31 Friday

Read the following paragraph and decide if the underlined parts have a capitalization error, a punctuation error, a spelling error, or no error.

Success in reading depends on using active strategies to <u>increase comprihension</u>. <u>Do you have</u>
                                                          1   2

<u>stratedgies that you use</u>. Before you read, do you organize your materials and tune in
          3

to the task? <u>As you read do you take notes and look up words?</u> <u>After you read do you</u>
                        4   5

review and use your new information to answer questions?

1. _____
2. _____
3. _____
4. _____
5. _____

Daily Language Review

Week 31 My Progress

How many did you get correct each day? Color the squares.

	Monday	Tuesday	Wednesday	Thursday	Friday
5					
4					
3					
2					
1					

Daily Language Review

WEEK 32 — Monday

Correct these sentences.

1. pebbles and bam bam are charesters in the movie the flint stones
_____

2. because it snowd mr ruiz the building manager cleared the walks
_____

Simile or metaphor?

3. The quiet surrounded her like a soft, downy comforter. _____

Circle the word that is not spelled correctly.

4. feeling   group   makings   natcheral   quarrelsome

What time is it?

5. The clock in the hallway chimed one, but there was no one about, and even the stars seemed to sleep under a thick blanket of clouds. _____

WEEK 32 — Tuesday

Write the possessive form.

1. uniforms of those band members _____

Correct these sentences.

2. homer spit is a peace of land that juts into kamishak bay from alaska
_____

3. the empress hotel in victoria british columbia has a lovey dinning room
_____

Synonyms, antonyms, or homophones?

4. pair, pare _____

Number these words in the correct alphabetical order.

5. ☐ breakage   ☐ breadwinner   ☐ breeze   ☐ brevity   ☐ breakfast

Daily Language Review

WEEK 32 Wednesday

Correct these sentences.

1. me and my brothers like to play monopoly on saturday after noons
   _____

2. eating a apple every day is suppose to keep the docter away
   _____

Write the two words that make up this contraction.

3. would've _____   _____

What part of speech is underlined in this sentence?

4. <u>Avoid</u> eating too many sweets. _____

Circle the word that does not belong.

5. plywood   oak   maple   birch   elm

WEEK 32 Thursday

Use this homophone pair in one sentence: *gate, gait*.

1. _____

If the guide words on a dictionary page are *dabble* and *damage*, which words would not be found on the page?

2. Dalmatian   dainty   dab   damask   daily

Correct these sentences.

3. once up on a time there was a king and a queen and a magnificant castel
   _____

4. pleeze put up you're umbrela after your out side the door
   _____

Rewrite the word *bank*, adding a prefix and a suffix.

5. _____

95

Daily Language Review

WEEK 32 Friday

Complete these sentences.

1. The best book I ever read was _____.

2. _____ is my favorite song of all time.

3. _____ was the best movie I saw this year.

4. I could read the poem _____ over and over again.

5. Yesterday, I watched _____ on television.

Daily Language Review

WEEK 32 My Progress

How many did you get correct each day? Color the squares.

	Monday	Tuesday	Wednesday	Thursday	Friday
5					
4					
3					
2					
1					

Daily Language Review

WEEK 33 Monday

Correct these sentences.

1. i use choclate bars marshmellows and crackers to make a tastey desert

2. the name of the deserts s'mores and you will want more after you're furst one

Write the base or root word.

3. standardization _____

4. conspiracy _____

Underline the adverb phrase in this sentence.

5. Take what she says with a grain of salt.

Daily Language Review

WEEK 33 Tuesday

Circle the complete predicate in this sentence.

1. Did Max snore last night?

Use context clues to determine the meaning of the bolded word.

2. The **vain** actor kept photos of himself all over the house.

Correct these sentences.

3. i believe that goldilocks was a trespaser announced the teacher

4. I agree with you're assessment replyed the student

Rewrite the word *scope*, adding a prefix.

5. _____

97

Daily Language Review

WEEK 33 Wednesday

Correct these sentences.

1. black widow spiders and mexican tarantula are faresome insexts

2. some times I wish I was a eagle soring threw the clear blew sky

Complete this analogy.

3. predator : prey :: lion : _____

What part of speech is the underlined word?

4. Suddenly the wind burst through the window and <u>slapped</u> the door closed.

5. When the mouse ran <u>across</u> the room, Carolyn stood on a chair and screamed.

Daily Language Review

WEEK 33 Thursday

Write the pronoun that would replace the underlined nouns in this sentence.

1. I mixed <u>carrots, peas, and mushrooms</u> in the pan. _____

Circle the word that does not belong in this group.

2. vertical   horizontal   square   perpendicular   parallel

Correct these sentences.

3. tonya said my legs go two sleep when i set on them

4. stephen said oh my legs go too sleep when im laying on the bed

What part of speech is the underlined word?

5. The books were <u>so</u> heavy that I almost dropped them. _____

Daily Language Review

Week 33 Friday

What do the underlined phrases mean?

1. When Scott sees my new bike, he'll be green with envy.

   _____

2. When it comes to swimming, Tony is head and shoulders above everyone else.

   _____

3. The coach thinks that the game is in the bag.

   _____

4. Classical music isn't my cup of tea.

   _____

5. Suzie was so excited, she let the cat out of the bag.

   _____

Daily Language Review

Week 33 My Progress

How many did you get correct each day? Color the squares.

	Monday	Tuesday	Wednesday	Thursday	Friday
5					
4					
3					
2					
1					

Daily Language Review

WEEK 34 — Monday

Correct these sentences.

1. charlie peter and tim we're late becuase they took there time

2. they had to go to the principles office an appologize to there teacher

Use context clues to determine the meaning of the bolded word.

3. Our teacher **enunciates** so that students who are learning English can understand her.

Circle the correct way to divide this word into syllables.

4. ri di cu le   rid ic ule   rid i cule   ri dic ule

When might you hear the following?

5. "Look under N for number 35." _____

WEEK 34 — Tuesday

Write a fact about *straight hair*.

1. _____

If the guide words on a dictionary page are *collate* and *collision*, which words would be on the page?

2. collarbone   collector   collapse   collage   college

Correct these sentences.

3. sue played soccor and was a cheer leader but she always made time for homework

4. because computers make finding facts easy they are a good source of infromation

Does the underlined adverb tell how, when, where, or to what extent?

5. Kittens can be <u>irritatingly</u> playful. _____

Daily Language Review

WEEK 34 Wednesday

Correct these sentences.

1. cuz ive never been back packing before i can't hardly weight to go
   _____

2. I putted sew many things in my pack that it ways fourty pounds
   _____

Write the abbreviation for *second*.

3. _____

Write the plural form of *mosquito*.

4. _____

Circle the words that are spelled correctly.

5. receive   ourselves   ownce   anoye   boundary

Daily Language Review

WEEK 34 Thursday

Write a common noun for this proper noun.

1. Martin Luther King, Jr. Day _____

Write the comparative and superlative forms of *good*.

2. Comparative: _____   Superlative: _____

Correct these sentences.

3. greyhound bus drivers are reposnible for many passengers they must be alert
   _____

4. mom has been buying soda hot dogs and buns she may have plans for sunday
   _____

What is the following person's job?

5. Mr. Lee checked the screens in front of him and spoke into his headset, "You are cleared to land."
   _____

Daily Language Review

WEEK 34 Friday

Choose the best word to complete each sentence.

1. Mrs. Riley is patient with everyone in her class, so she deserves the _____ Award.
   Procrastinator   Anxiety   Forbearance   Cantankerous

2. He was _____ when his science fair project collapsed as the judge looked at it.
   chagrined   thrilled   fortunate   fulfilled

3. Frannie took her bow amid the applause and _____ of her fellow musicians.
   disapproval   acclaim   scorn   alarm

4. The trail mix will provide _____ for the hike.
   adornment   earnings   sustenance   bulk

5. She hopes to _____ her progress so that she can complete the course in half the time.
   delay   furnish   dissolve   accelerate

Daily Language Review

WEEK 34 My Progress

How many did you get correct each day? Color the squares.

	Monday	Tuesday	Wednesday	Thursday	Friday
5					
4					
3					
2					
1					

Daily Language Review

Week 35 Monday

Correct these sentences.

1. impatient my lab partner ask when do you think youll compleat the project

_____

2. i replyed ill be done as soon as i finish the research compose my ideas and print it out

_____

Complete this analogy.

3. penguin : bird :: pizza : _____

Underline the complete subject of each sentence.

4. Thirty-two hungry, rowdy kindergartners burst through the lunchroom doors.

5. When she was asked to give her phone number, the new girl answered, "I haven't learned it."

Daily Language Review

Week 35 Tuesday

Does this word have a suffix, a prefix, both, or none?

1. extraordinary _____

Write a word that would belong in this category.

2. Denver   Sacramento   Austin   Frankfort   _____

Correct these sentences.

3. on saturday june 5 ann will drive from arlington virginia to champaign illinois

_____

4. tricias swiming imporved so much she moved from the novice to the intermmediate class

_____

Circle the correct way to divide this word into syllables.

5. rev o lu tion ar y   re vo lu tion ar y   rev o lut ion ar y   re vol u tion ar y

Daily Language Review

WEEK 35 Wednesday

Correct these sentences.

1. how is sking and snowboreding different ask simons uncle

   _____

2. tulips roses and lilacs line grannys pathway it smells like a flour shop

   _____

Write the present form and the past participle of the verb *did*.

3. Present form: _____   Past participle: _____

Circle the words that are not spelled correctly.

4. addresses   busineses   familys   countries   flies

Synonyms, antonyms, or homophones?

5. mature, develop _____

WEEK 35 Thursday

Write the comparative and superlative adjectives of the word *beautiful*.

1. Comparative: _____   Superlative: _____

Circle the adjectives in this sentence.

2. Aunt Carol's sixtieth birthday party was an exciting celebration of her many friends.

Correct these sentences.

3. somethings fishy exclaimmed the detective ill check it out

   _____

4. I wish that I was tall like my friend john so then I could slamdunk the ball

   _____

Explain what the underlined idiom in this sentence means.

5. I've been saving for rollerblades for over a year, but I finally <u>see a light at the end of the tunnel</u>.

   _____

Daily Language Review

WEEK 35 Friday

Label the subject or subjects and verb of each sentence.

1. This summer, my brother and I would like to learn to scuba dive.

   Subject(s): _____ Verb: _____

2. When I was mowing the lawn, a little frog hopped out of the grass.

   Subject(s): _____ Verb: _____

3. A sudden storm took the campers by surprise.

   Subject(s): _____ Verb: _____

4. I've never seen a purple cow.

   Subject(s): _____ Verb: _____

5. Misha's elderly aunt and her cat live down the street.

   Subject(s): _____ Verb: _____

Daily Language Review

WEEK 35 My Progress

How many did you get correct each day? Color the squares.

	Monday	Tuesday	Wednesday	Thursday	Friday
5					
4					
3					
2					
1					

Daily Language Review
Week 36 Monday

Correct these sentences.

1. when water got hot it change in to water vaper this process is called evaporation

2. when water vaper got cold it change in to a liqid this process is called condensation

Are the underlined words a common noun or a proper noun?

3. My favorite treat is a <u>caramel apple</u> from the Chocolate Factory. _____

Metaphor or simile?

4. Mom has had her new washer repaired three times. She bought a lemon!
   _____

Circle the word with the most syllables.

5. nourishment   humiliation   persevere   courageously

Daily Language Review
Week 36 Tuesday

Circle the words that are spelled correctly.

1. awkward   allready   daughter   brought   althouh   stalke

Correct these sentences.

2. horton the elefant was determine when he said on birds egg and hatches it

3. do you think dr seusss grinch wood like to eat green eggs and ham

Interrogative or declarative?

4. Would you like me to check the tires? _____

5. The astronauts repaired the space station. _____

Daily Language Review

WEEK 36 Wednesday

Correct these sentences.

1. I play the piccolo doug explained because its easyer to carrie a piccolo than a tuba

2. after the movie jason ask do you think scientist will clon dna to create a living dinosaur

Write a fact about *vegetables*.

3. _____

Synonyms, antonyms, or homophones?

4. grand, large _____

5. temporary, permanent _____

Daily Language Review

WEEK 36 Thursday

If the guide words on a dictionary page are *manicure* and *mantel*, which words would not be found on the page?

1. man-made   maniac   mannerism   mantilla   mantle

Rewrite this word, adding a suffix.

2. imagine _____

Correct these sentences.

3. must I take a water filter on the back packing trip ask bill I will carry water in my canteen

4. you will be glad you did take the filter if you need more water the scout master answer

Write an alliterative phrase about *dogs*.

5. _____

Daily Language Review
WEEK 36 Friday

Read the following paragraph and decide if the underlined parts have a capitalization error, a punctuation error, a spelling error, a noun/verb agreement error, or no error.

<u>Solids, liquids and gases</u> are all <u>conducters of sound</u>, but the speed of sound is different for each type
        1   2   3

of material. <u>Sound waves travels much faster</u> through solids and <u>liquides</u> than through gases.
                                  4   5

1. _____
2. _____
3. _____
4. _____
5. _____

Daily Language Review
WEEK 36 My Progress

How many did you get correct each day? Color the squares.

	Monday	Tuesday	Wednesday	Thursday	Friday
5					
4					
3					
2					
1					

Good for You

You have successfully completed

Daily Language Review

Sentence Editing Checklist

Use this checklist to help correct the daily sentence.

 Does each sentence begin with a capital letter?

 Does each sentence end with a period, a question mark, or an exclamation point?

 Do names of people, places, and other proper nouns, such as books, songs, and poems, begin with a capital letter?

 Did I use a period in abbreviations and initials?

 Did I use apostrophes to show possession (Anna's desk) and in contractions (isn't)?

 Did I choose the correct word?
- homophones (to, two, too)
- verbs (is, are)
- pronouns (he, him)

 Did I check for spelling errors?

 Did I place commas where they are needed?
    words in a series
    addresses, dates
    dialogue
    compound sentences
    introductory phrases

 Did I underline the names of books, magazines, movies, and plays?

 Did I use quotation marks
    to show the exact words being spoken?
    around the names of poems, songs, and short stories?